Digesting
How we fuel the body

Contributors

Author: **Angela Royston MA** has written over 100 books for children on a range of subjects, including human biology, plants and animals, transport and the environment.

Series consultant: **Richard Walker BSc PhD PGCE** taught biology, science and health education for several years before becoming a full-time writer. He is a foremost author and consultant specializing in books for adults and children on human biology, health and natural history. He is the author of *Heart: How the blood gets around the body, Making Life: How we reproduce and grow, Muscles: How we move and exercise* and *Brain: Our body's nerve centre* in this series.

Advisory panel

1 Heart: How the blood gets around the body
P M Schofield MD FRCP FICA FACC FESC is Consultant Cardiologist at Papworth Hospital, Cambridge

2 Skeleton: Our body's framework
R N Villar MS FRCS is Consultant Orthopaedic Surgeon at Cambridge BUPA Lea Hospital and Addenbrooke's Hospital, Cambridge

3 Digesting: How we fuel the body
J O Hunter FRCP is Director of the Gastroenterology Research Unit, Addenbrooke's Hospital, Cambridge

4 Making Life: How we reproduce and grow
Jane MacDougall MD MRCOG
is Consultant Obstetrician and Gynaecologist at the Rosie Maternity Hospital, Addenbrooke's NHS Trust, Cambridge

5 Breathing: How we use air
Mark Slade MA MBBS MRCP is Senior Registrar, Department of Respiratory Medicine, Addenbrooke's Hospital, Cambridge

6 Senses: How we connect with the world
Peter Garrard MA MRCP is Medical Research Council Fellow and Honorary Specialist Registrar, Neurology Department, Addenbrooke's Hospital, Cambridge

7 Muscles: How we move and exercise
Jumbo Jenner MD FRCP is Consultant, and **R T Kavanagh MD MRCP** is Senior Registrar, Department of Rheumatology, Addenbrooke's Hospital, Cambridge

8 Brain: Our body's nerve centre
Peter Garrard MA MRCP is Medical Research Council Fellow and Honorary Specialist Registrar, Neurology Department, Addenbrooke's Hospital, Cambridge

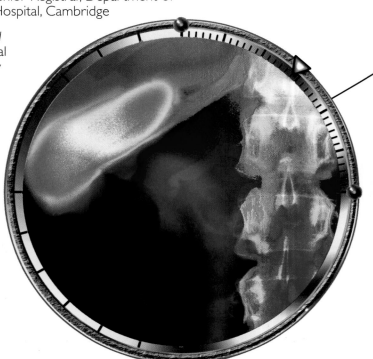

Digesting
How we fuel the body

Angela Royston

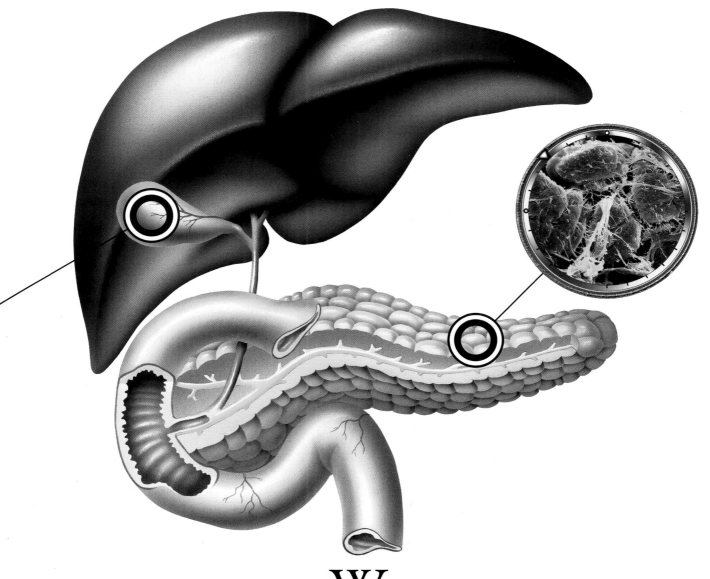

W
FRANKLIN WATTS
NEW YORK•LONDON•SYDNEY

ABOUT THIS BOOK

First published in 1998

Franklin Watts
96 Leonard Street
London EC2A 4RH

Franklin Watts Australia
14 Mars Road
Lane Cove
NSW 2066

© Franklin Watts 1998

0 7496 3072 8

Dewey Decimal Classification Number: 612.3

A CIP catalogue record for this book is
available from the British Library

Printed in Belgium

Produced for Franklin Watts
by Miles Kelly Publishing
Unit 11
The Bardfield Centre
Great Bardfield
Essex
CM7 4SL

Designed by Full Steam Ahead

Illustrated by Mike Atkinson and
Guy Smith, Mainline Design

Artwork commissioned by
Branka Surla

Under the Microscope uses micro-photography to allow you to see right inside the human body.

The camera acts as a microscope, looking at unseen parts of the body and zooming in on the body's cells at work. Some micro-photographs are magnified hundreds of times, others thousands of times. They have been dramatically coloured to bring details into crisp focus, and are linked to clear and accurate illustrations that fit them in context inside the body.

New words are explained the first time that they are used, and can also be checked in the glossary at the back of the book.

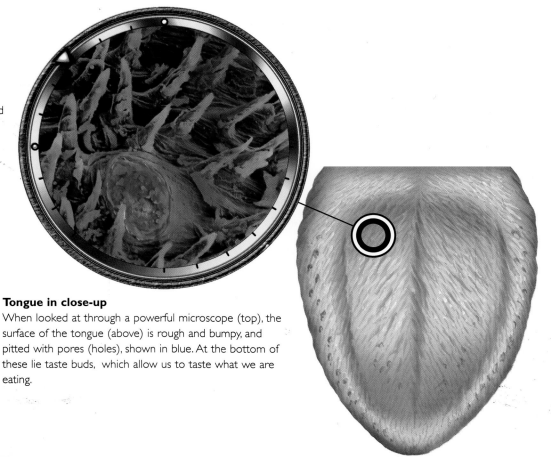

Tongue in close-up
When looked at through a powerful microscope (top), the surface of the tongue (above) is rough and bumpy, and pitted with pores (holes), shown in blue. At the bottom of these lie taste buds, which allow us to taste what we are eating.

CONTENTS

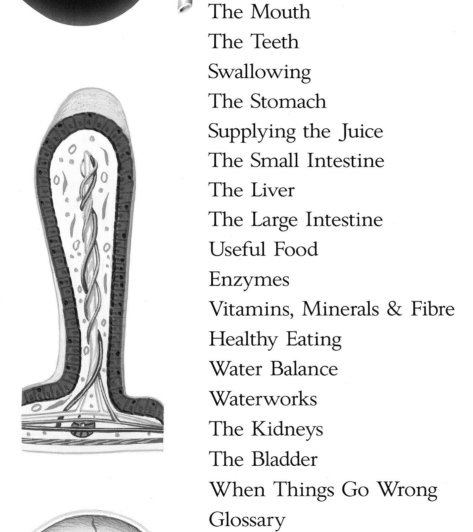

INTRODUCTION

Adult teeth
This special type of X-ray – called a CT scan – shows a complete set of teeth in an adult's lower jaw. We use our teeth to chew up food prior to swallowing.

When you eat a meal, you are sending the food on an epic journey through the digestive tract. This long tube joins your mouth to your stomach and then coils and winds its way through the abdomen to the anus. In fact, you can think of your body like a hollow bead. The digestive tract is the long hole through the centre.

Only part of the meal – the indigestible part that leaves the body as faeces – will complete the whole journey through the digestive tract. Most of the meal is digested. The food is chemically changed, then taken inside the body and used to nourish it in several ways. Food provides energy for every part of the body – such as the muscles, eyes, heart and brain – to do its job. Food also keeps the body warm and provides all the special chemicals you need to grow and stay healthy.

Millions of tiny cells make up each part of the body. Many of these cells do not live for more than a few weeks or months, so the body is constantly making new cells to replace the old ones. It gets the energy and materials it needs to do this from food.

Stomach gland
This enormous pit (right) is actually the entrance to one of the stomach's many glands, as seen by a scanning electron microscope. Stomach glands produce a liquid that helps digest food.

Large intestine
Passing up, across and down the abdomen, the tubular large intestine, seen on the left in a coloured X-ray, forms the last part of the digestive system. The backbone can be seen in the background.

Inside the liver
A view inside the human liver, revealed in the micrograph above, shows not only liver cells but also blood cells from blood flowing through the liver. The liver processes food after it has been digested.

7

FOOD -THE BODY'S FUEL

All the energy your body needs comes from food. After the food you eat has been digested, the nutrients it contained are taken by the blood to every living cell in the body.

One of these nutrients is glucose — a kind of sugar. Cells use glucose to provide energy rather like a car burns petrol. Your body needs energy to function all the time, even when you are asleep. The more active you are, the more energy you need. Sports such as running and swimming are among the most energetic activities.

People who do jobs that involve a lot of hard physical work, such as builders and dancers, use more energy in their daily lives than people who work sitting down in a bank or office. Young people burn up a lot of energy running about and playing sports. Teenagers need more food than adults, for growth and development. But older people, even those who are still active, need less energy and therefore less food.

Energy in food is measured in units called kilojoules or Calories (4.2kJ = 1 Cal).

Full of energy
Your body demands more energy when you are exercising than when you are resting. Regular exercise makes you fitter and more likely to be healthy.

Energetic activities
The body uses energy all the time, whatever you are doing. The figures given here show how much energy you would need if you performed each activity for an hour. Running and swimming use the most energy, but even sleeping uses some.

READING 273 kJ/HR (65 CAL/HR)

SLEEPING 252 kJ/HR (60 CAL/HR)

EATING 294 kJ/HR (70 CAL/HR)

Supplying the cell

When digested, some of the foods we eat are turned into glucose, the simple substance that provides energy for living. The blood carries a constant supply of oxygen and glucose to all parts of the body. Inside each cell, oxygen and glucose combine to release energy, with carbon dioxide and water as waste products.

Energy users

Some parts of the body use more energy than other parts. When you are doing something active, such as running, swimming or dancing, the muscles use the most.

OXYGEN

GLUCOSE

ENERGY

Nucleus (control centre of cell)

Mitochondrion (power plant of cell, where energy is released)

Fat 9%

Kidneys 8%

Other 13%

Heart 11%

Brain 19%

Liver 20%

Muscle 20%

WALKING 1083 KJ/HR (246 CAL/HR)

SWIMMING 1612 KJ/HR (384 CAL/HR)

RUNNING 2419 KJ/HR (576 CAL/HR)

THE DIGESTION MACHINE

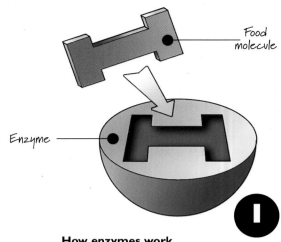

Food molecule

Enzyme

How enzymes work
Enzymes are chemicals that play an important part in digestion. They act as catalysts: that is, they speed up the breakdown of large food molecules into smaller ones. This sequence shows how they work.

Your body can't use food in the form that you swallow it. The digestive system uses mechanical processes (chewing and churning) and chemical processes (enzymes) to break food down into smaller and smaller pieces.

In the mouth, food is chopped and ground by the teeth and moistened with saliva. In the stomach, it is churned around into a mushy soup and mixed with digestive juices. Saliva and digestive juices contain substances called enzymes. Enzymes are chemicals that attack the food and help to digest it. As the food being digested passes out of the stomach and into the small intestine, more enzymes continue to break it down into separate particles small enough to pass through the walls of the intestine into the blood.

Each lump or bolus of food being digested is moved along the digestive tract by a process called peristalsis. Muscles in the walls of the digestive tube squeeze together behind the bolus to push it along. When all the nutrients have been absorbed from the food, the bulk that is left is passed out of the body.

A large food molecule fits precisely into a part of the enzyme just like a key fits into a lock (1). Once it is in place inside the enzyme (2), the large food molecule breaks down into smaller parts.

Smaller food molecules

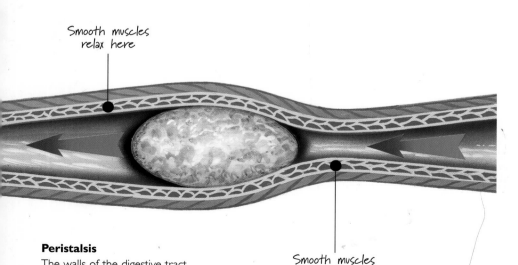

Smooth muscles relax here

Peristalsis
The walls of the digestive tract contain sheets of smooth muscles. They contract behind the food and move it along, rather like squeezing toothpaste out of a tube.

Smooth muscles contract here

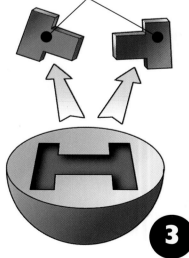

The smaller food molecules move away from the enzyme (3). The enzyme itself – having acted as a chemical digester – remains unchanged, and is ready to help break down more large food molecules.

Long journey of a meal

Food may take 24 hours or more to travel through the whole digestive tract — the 9.5-metre (31-foot) long tube that joins the mouth to the anus, where waste leaves the body.

Food pipe
The oesophagus pushes the food from the mouth into the stomach.

Small meets large
This micrograph shows where the lining of the small intestine (blue) meets that of the large intestine (yellow).

Mouth
The teeth and jaw muscles work together to break up bite-sized lumps of food into smaller ones that can be swallowed.

Liver
This large organ produces bile, a liquid that helps to break down fats. The liver also processes digested food brought to it in the blood.

Bile store
Bile is stored in the gall bladder until it is needed. Then it is squirted into the first part of the small intestine.

Small intestine
Enzymes in the digestive juices break up food particles into simple molecules that pass through the walls of the small intestine and are absorbed into the blood.

Large intestine
Food that is not absorbed passes on through the large intestine. Water is absorbed back into the blood and the waste material becomes more solid.

Stomach
This stretchy bag stores food for about four hours. While the food is in the stomach it is churned into a mushy soup.

Pancreas
The pancreas produces digestive juices that flow into the small intestine.

Getting rid of waste
Waste is stored in the rectum until the body is ready to expel it through the anus.

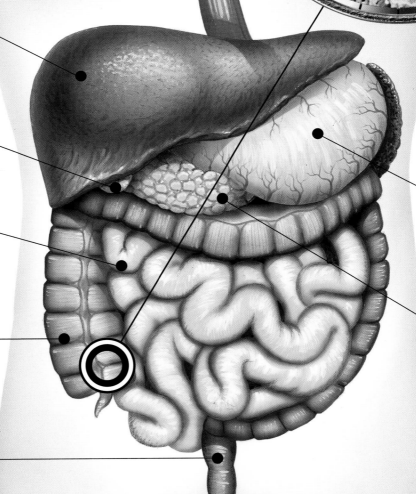

THE MOUTH

The digestive process begins as soon as you put food into your mouth. Teeth break the food into smaller pieces, and the salivary glands pump out saliva which the tongue mixes with the food to make it soft and mushy.

While the tongue, teeth and the inside of the mouth turn the food into a mushy ball, taste buds on the tongue and in the mouth tell you how good the food tastes. Saliva has several jobs to do. It lets you taste what you are eating, by taking small amounts of dissolved food to taste buds in your tongue. It is slightly antiseptic, so it can kill some of the germs that may be in the food. Saliva also contains an enzyme that changes starch in the food into sugars. The jaw muscles work hard as you chew, moving the lower teeth up and down against the upper teeth. The upper jaw does not move at all.

A cool lick
Part of the pleasure of eating is the way food tastes and feels in your mouth. The lips are very sensitive to heat and cold.

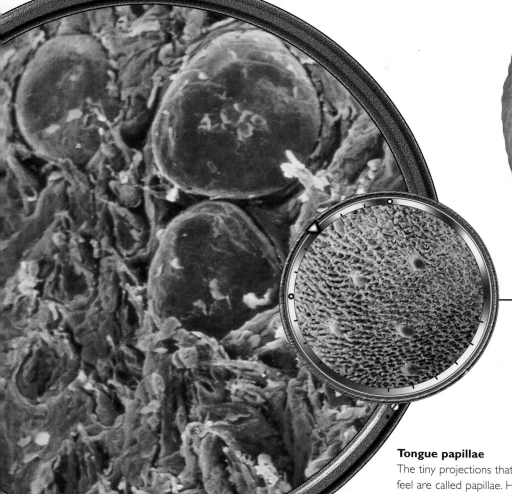

Bumpy muscle
The tongue is a muscular flap that you can move in all directions, to help in chewing and in talking. Its rough, bumpy surface lets you taste the food as it moves around your mouth.

Tongue papillae
The tiny projections that give the tongue its rough feel are called papillae. Here you can see the round papillae that carry the taste buds that enable you to taste food. The spiky papillae allow you to feel food and help the tongue to grip food during chewing.

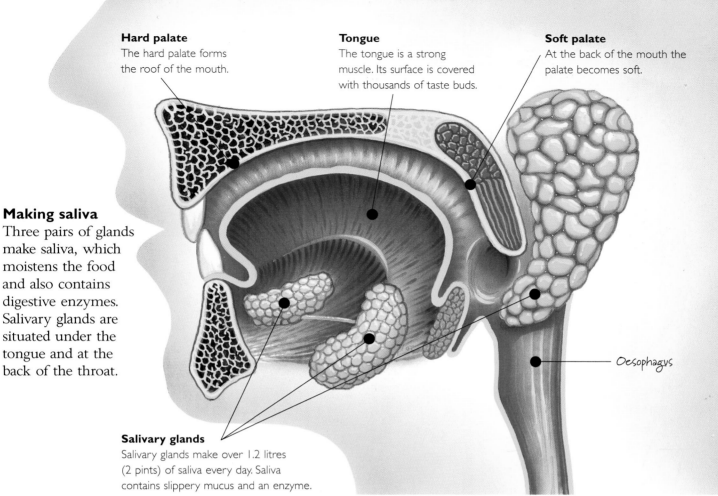

Hard palate
The hard palate forms the roof of the mouth.

Tongue
The tongue is a strong muscle. Its surface is covered with thousands of taste buds.

Soft palate
At the back of the mouth the palate becomes soft.

Making saliva
Three pairs of glands make saliva, which moistens the food and also contains digestive enzymes. Salivary glands are situated under the tongue and at the back of the throat.

Oesophagus

Salivary glands
Salivary glands make over 1.2 litres (2 pints) of saliva every day. Saliva contains slippery mucus and an enzyme.

Taste bud
Taste buds, such as the one shown (right), are found on the sides and top of tongue papillae. The round, dark area is a taste pore, the opening to the taste bud. Dissolved food entering the taste pore is detected by the taste bud below it.

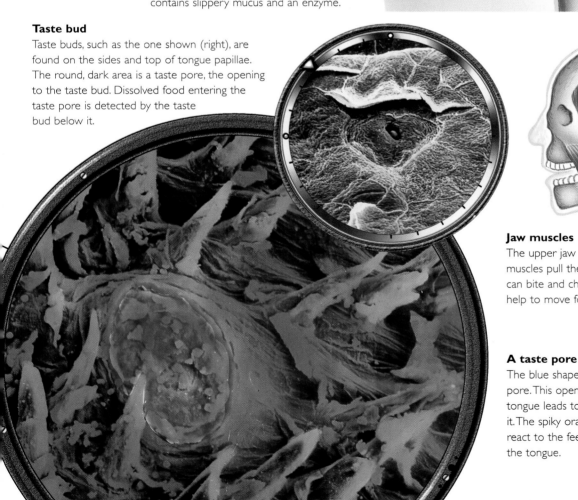

Jaw muscles
The upper jaw cannot move, but powerful muscles pull the lower jaw upwards so you can bite and chew. Muscles in the cheeks also help to move food around the mouth.

A taste pore
The blue shape in the centre is a taste pore. This opening in the surface of the tongue leads to taste buds that lie just below it. The spiky orange tips around the pore react to the feel of food as it moves across the tongue.

THE TEETH

Different-shaped teeth have different jobs to do.

The chisel-shaped incisors at the front of the mouth cut bite-sized chunks out of the food. The pointed canines grip and pierce the food. The large, flat-topped premolars and molars at the back of the mouth grind the food into small pieces.

Humans have only two sets of teeth throughout their life — some animals have many more. The first set of 20 teeth, called milk teeth, develop in the jaw before birth. The first tooth pushes its way through the gum when the baby is about six months old, and the rest follow, one by one, over the next two years.

Below them, 32 larger teeth are growing in the jaw. Between the ages of seven and 14 they gradually push the milk teeth out.

Biting
The large sharp teeth at the front of the mouth slice into the apple. Together, the top and bottom teeth make a pincer-like movement and bite off a mouthful.

Inside a tooth
A tooth has two parts: the crown, above the gum, and the root below it. The crown is coated with enamel. Under the enamel is dentine, which is as hard as bone. Below this is the pulp cavity, which contains blood vessels and nerves.

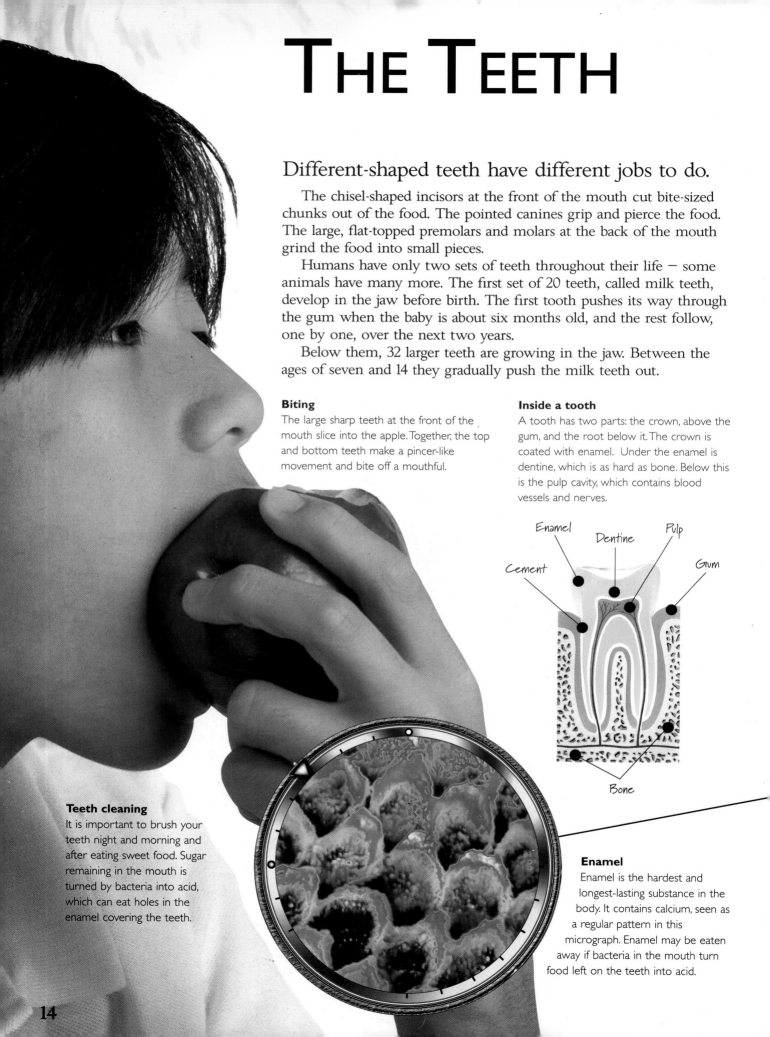

Enamel   Dentine   Pulp

Cement   Gum

Bone

Teeth cleaning
It is important to brush your teeth night and morning and after eating sweet food. Sugar remaining in the mouth is turned by bacteria into acid, which can eat holes in the enamel covering the teeth.

Enamel
Enamel is the hardest and longest-lasting substance in the body. It contains calcium, seen as a regular pattern in this micrograph. Enamel may be eaten away if bacteria in the mouth turn food left on the teeth into acid.

A full set of permanent teeth

Permanent teeth grow from the upper and lower jawbones and begin to form even before you are born. Teeth chew and mash up food into smaller pieces so that it can be swallowed. Each kind of tooth works in a different way.

Two sets of teeth
This X-ray shows a permanent tooth growing below the milk tooth. The root of the milk tooth begins to dissolve so that the tooth falls out to make room for the new, permanent tooth.

Slicers
There are eight incisors. They have wide, sharp edges that slice into food.

Grippers
There are four pointed canines, one at each corner of the mouth. They grip the food and tear off a bite.

Grinders
There are 12 large square molars. Their surface is bumpy and they grind against each other like millstones to reduce the food to a pulp.

Tearers
There are eight premolars. They have two peaks that tear and grind food.

Wisdom teeth
The four molars at the very back of the mouth are called wisdom teeth because they do not appear until you are adult, when you are supposed to be wise. Sometimes they don't come up at all!

SWALLOWING

Swallowing takes just one or two seconds. When the mouthful of food has been reduced to a soft, mushy ball, called a bolus, the tongue moves it to the back of the mouth.

As soon as the bolus touches the soft palate, you swallow it and the food passes into the throat. At the same time 'trap doors', called the epiglottis, slam shut across the inner entrance to your nose and windpipe to make sure the food goes the right way – down the oesophagus into the stomach, not down the windpipe into the lungs.

You don't have to think about swallowing – it is an automatic action called a reflex action – and when something goes wrong, another reflex action makes you choke. A morsel of food that 'goes down the wrong way' into the windpipe because the epiglottis has not shut completely, is automatically forced out by violent coughing. A crumb lodged in the throat can also be coughed up or swept into the oesophagus by a drink of water.

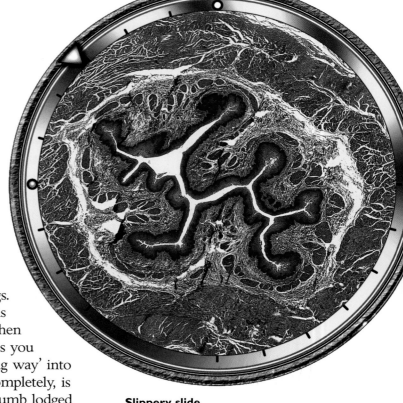

Slippery slide
This section cut across the oesophagus shows its muscular wall. The inside of the oesophagus is coated with mucus to help the food slide down.

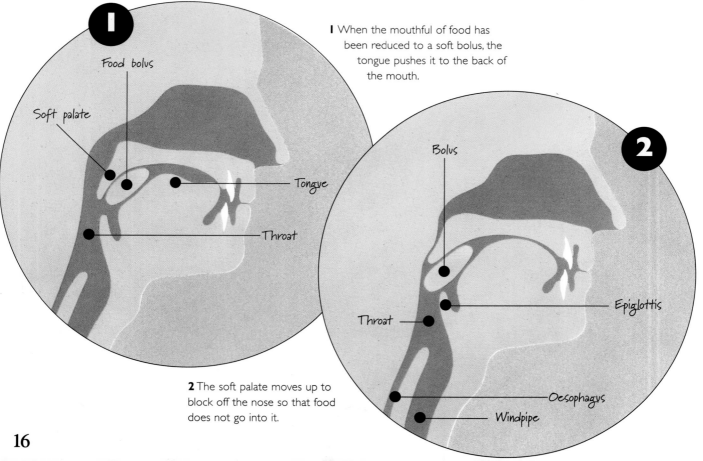

1 When the mouthful of food has been reduced to a soft bolus, the tongue pushes it to the back of the mouth.

Food bolus

Soft palate

Tongue

Throat

Bolus

Throat

Epiglottis

Oesophagus

Windpipe

2 The soft palate moves up to block off the nose so that food does not go into it.

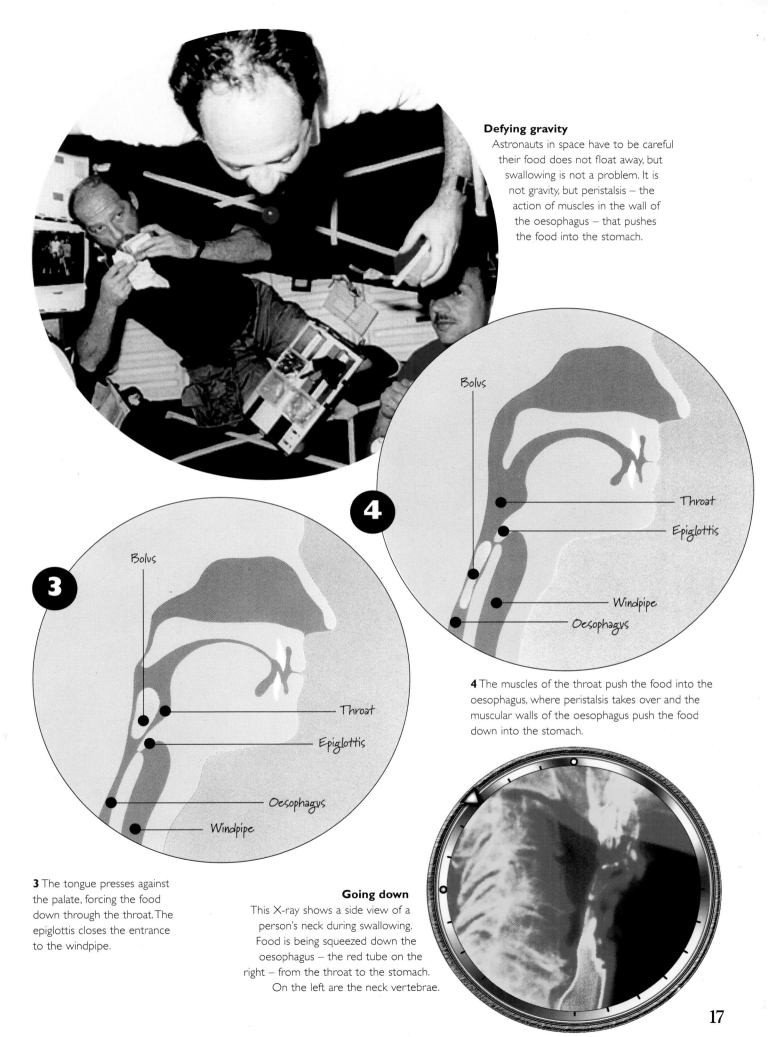

Defying gravity
Astronauts in space have to be careful their food does not float away, but swallowing is not a problem. It is not gravity, but peristalsis – the action of muscles in the wall of the oesophagus – that pushes the food into the stomach.

Bolus

4

Throat

Epiglottis

Windpipe

Oesophagus

4 The muscles of the throat push the food into the oesophagus, where peristalsis takes over and the muscular walls of the oesophagus push the food down into the stomach.

Bolus

3

Throat

Epiglottis

Oesophagus

Windpipe

3 The tongue presses against the palate, forcing the food down through the throat. The epiglottis closes the entrance to the windpipe.

Going down
This X-ray shows a side view of a person's neck during swallowing. Food is being squeezed down the oesophagus – the red tube on the right – from the throat to the stomach. On the left are the neck vertebrae.

THE STOMACH

Five seconds after being swallowed, the mouthful of food enters the stomach, where it will stay for up to four hours. The stomach is a J-shaped bag that expands to store food.

The stomach walls contain strong muscles. They squeeze and churn the food, mixing it with gastric (stomach) juices to form a thick mush called chyme. Gastric juices pour into the stomach from glands in the stomach's lining. These juices contain enzymes and hydrochloric acid (this is so strong that it could dissolve the metal zinc). The acid kills off most of the germs that may be in the food. The stomach itself is protected from the action of enzymes and acid by a thick layer of slimy mucus, but even so, half a million cells of the stomach lining die and must be replaced every minute.

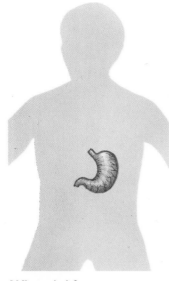

Where is it?
The stomach is a J-shaped bag that lies just below the ribs on the left side of the abdomen.

Belching
Belching is generally caused by eating too fast and swallowing air, or by drinking carbonated (fizzy) drink. The gas and air escape back up the oesophagus when you belch.

Stomach exit
A valve called the pyloric sphincter (right) controls the exit from the stomach. It stops food leaving the stomach until it has been churned into a thick liquid.

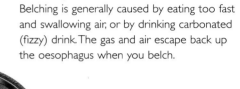

The stomach wall
The stomach lining is called the mucosa. Below its deeply pitted and slimy surface are thousands of glands, which together produce about 3 litres (5 pints) of gastric juices a day. Below the stomach lining are layers of muscles, which pull the walls of the stomach in different directions, squeezing the food inside.

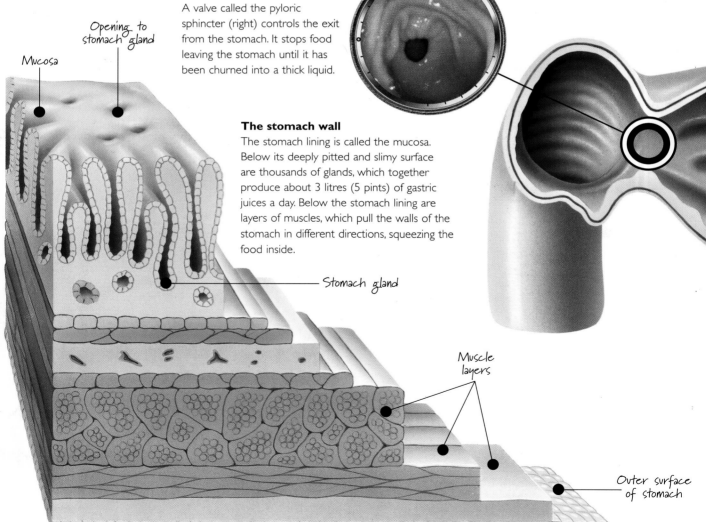

Opening to stomach gland

Mucosa

Stomach gland

Muscle layers

Outer surface of stomach

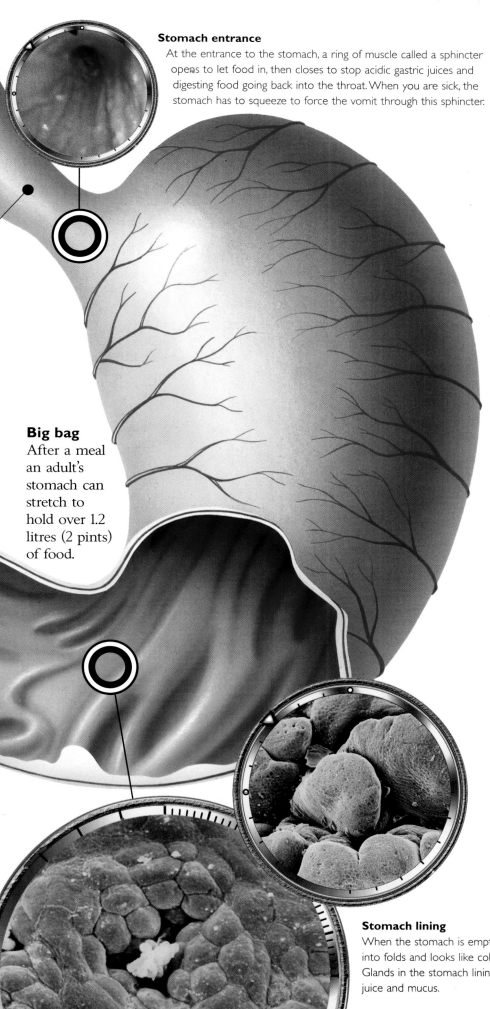

Stomach entrance

At the entrance to the stomach, a ring of muscle called a sphincter opens to let food in, then closes to stop acidic gastric juices and digesting food going back into the throat. When you are sick, the stomach has to squeeze to force the vomit through this sphincter.

Big bag

After a meal an adult's stomach can stretch to hold over 1.2 litres (2 pints) of food.

What happens to the food in your stomach

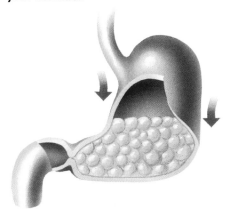

1 Each mouthful of food reaches the stomach as a soft bolus of chewed food. The more you eat, the more your stomach stretches.

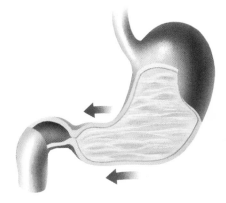

2 For an hour or two, the muscles in the stomach wall mash the food and mix it with acid and enzymes until it resembes a thick soup. This is called chyme.

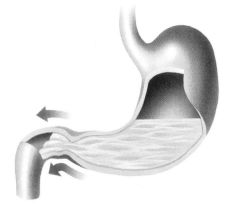

3 Chyme is forced bit by bit through the pyloric sphincter at the exit from the stomach, and into the small intestine. The stomach shrinks again to its usual size.

Stomach lining

When the stomach is empty the lining is relaxed into folds and looks like cobblestones (above). Glands in the stomach lining (left) produce gastric juice and mucus.

SUPPLYING THE JUICE

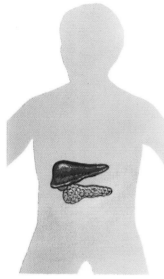

Spurt by spurt, chyme is squeezed from the acid environment of the stomach into the small intestine. Here, the pancreas and gall bladder immediately squirt it with digestive juices.

Stomach acids would destroy most enzymes, so the juice produced by the pancreas is alkaline, the opposite of acid. It mixes with the chyme to neutralize (cancel out) the acid. Then enzymes in the pancreatic juice can get to work. They break down large molecules into smaller ones.

The gall bladder squirts bile on to the chyme in the small intestine. This green liquid is made in the liver. It acts on fats like washing-up liquid, breaking them down into tiny droplets so they too can be worked upon by enzymes.

Where are they?
The pancreas and gall bladder lie just below the liver, close to the stomach and the duodenum, the first section of the small intestine.

The pancreas at work
These cells in the pancreas (right and below) produce digestive enzymes. The enzymes are carried by a duct (tube) to the small intestine.

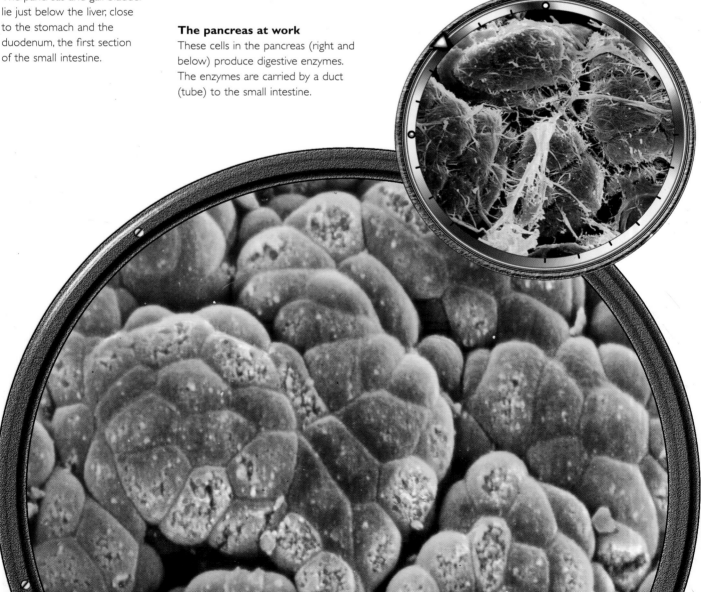

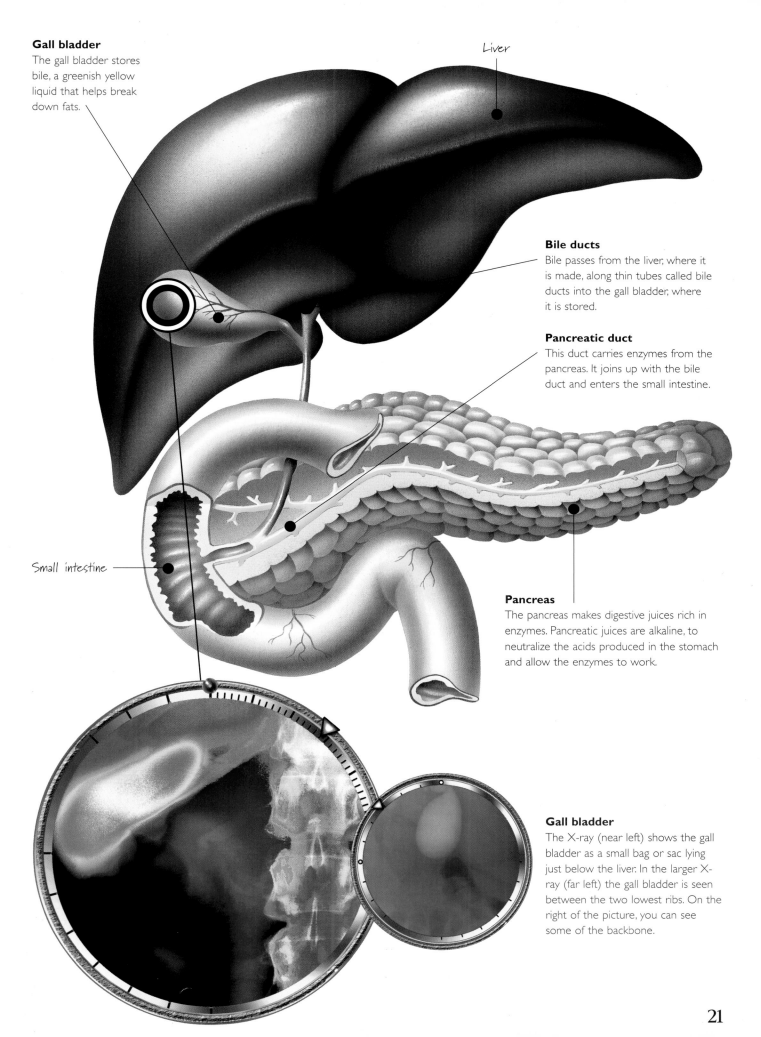

Gall bladder
The gall bladder stores bile, a greenish yellow liquid that helps break down fats.

Liver

Bile ducts
Bile passes from the liver, where it is made, along thin tubes called bile ducts into the gall bladder, where it is stored.

Pancreatic duct
This duct carries enzymes from the pancreas. It joins up with the bile duct and enters the small intestine.

Small intestine

Pancreas
The pancreas makes digestive juices rich in enzymes. Pancreatic juices are alkaline, to neutralize the acids produced in the stomach and allow the enzymes to work.

Gall bladder
The X-ray (near left) shows the gall bladder as a small bag or sac lying just below the liver. In the larger X-ray (far left) the gall bladder is seen between the two lowest ribs. On the right of the picture, you can see some of the backbone.

THE SMALL INTESTINE

Most digestion takes place in the small intestine. Digestive juices containing enzymes are secreted (leak) from its walls. These juices help the digestive juices from the pancreas and bile from the gall bladder to finish the job of breaking down food into simple molecules.

Simple food molecules are absorbed through the walls of the small intestine and into the blood, which transports them to the liver for processing. These simple molecules include glucose (from carbohydrate digestion), amino acids (from protein digestion) and fatty acids (from fat digestion). The sludgy remains of undigested food are then squeezed out of the small intestine and into the large intestine.

An adult's small intestine is 7 metres (22 feet) long. The internal surface area of the small intestine is made even bigger by many folds lined with millions of tiny finger-like villi that resemble the pile on a towel. Villi absorb digested food from the small intestine. Each villus is no more than 0.5 millimetres long, and covered with even smaller microvilli. These increase its surface area and absorbency still further.

Where is it?
The small intestine is coiled inside the lower part of the abdomen.

Microvilli
This hugely magnified micrograph of the wall of a villus shows that it is lined with thousands of microvilli, rather like the bristles on a brush. The microvilli increase the surface area through which nutrients can be absorbed.

A view through the small intestine
The wall of the intestine has two layers of smooth muscle. This moves the chyme along in slow, peristaltic waves. The small intestine is lined with millions of tiny finger-like villi. Nutrients are absorbed through them into the bloodstream.

Smooth muscle

Villus

Microvilli

Inside a villus
Molecules of digested food are so small that they pass through the cells lining the villus and into the blood vessels inside.

Blood vessels

Folds inside the small intestine, covered with villi

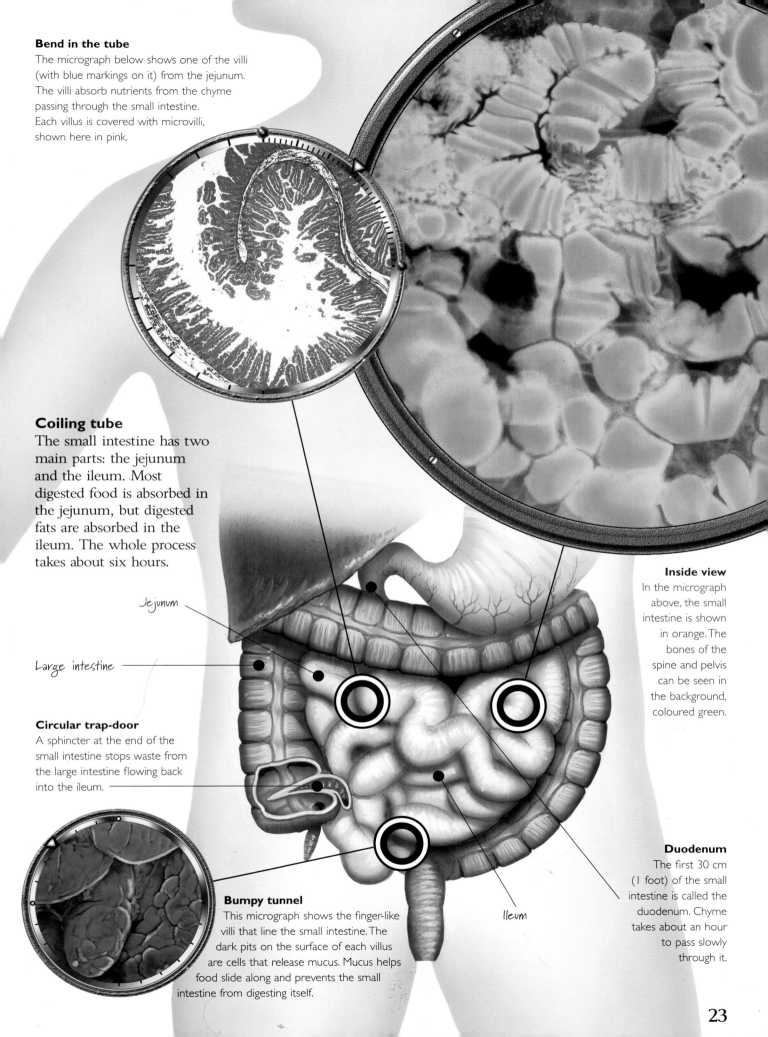

Bend in the tube
The micrograph below shows one of the villi (with blue markings on it) from the jejunum. The villi absorb nutrients from the chyme passing through the small intestine. Each villus is covered with microvilli, shown here in pink.

Coiling tube
The small intestine has two main parts: the jejunum and the ileum. Most digested food is absorbed in the jejunum, but digested fats are absorbed in the ileum. The whole process takes about six hours.

Jejunum

Large intestine

Circular trap-door
A sphincter at the end of the small intestine stops waste from the large intestine flowing back into the ileum.

Bumpy tunnel
This micrograph shows the finger-like villi that line the small intestine. The dark pits on the surface of each villus are cells that release mucus. Mucus helps food slide along and prevents the small intestine from digesting itself.

Inside view
In the micrograph above, the small intestine is shown in orange. The bones of the spine and pelvis can be seen in the background, coloured green.

Duodenum
The first 30 cm (1 foot) of the small intestine is called the duodenum. Chyme takes about an hour to pass slowly through it.

Ileum

THE LIVER

As soon as glucose molecules and other nutrients pass into the blood, they are taken to the liver to be processed. The liver monitors the amount of energy-giving glucose in the blood.

If there is more glucose than the body needs, the liver changes the extra into glycogen and stores it. As the body burns up glucose energy, the liver raids its store of glycogen and changes it back into glucose to keep you going.

The liver is also a waste disposal unit. As blood passes through it, it filters out excess amino acids (nutrients from protein-rich foods such as meat and beans) and changes them into urea, which leaves the body in urine. The liver breaks down worn-out red blood cells, and cleanses the blood of poisons taken in by the body, such as drugs and pesticides. These are turned into harmless substances that leave the body in urine.

Amazingly, unless you are actively moving about, one quarter of all your blood is in the liver being cleansed and re-stocked with energy-supplying glucose.

Where is it?

The liver, the largest organ in the body, lies just below the ribs in the top right-hand corner of the abdomen.

Liver cells

The liver is made up of liver cells – or hepatocytes – (coloured red-brown in the micrograph below, right). Liver cells have many functions, including the production of bile, a liquid that carries waste away from the liver and helps digest fats in the small intestine. Bile is drained from the liver along tiny bile canals, shown in the micrograph top right.

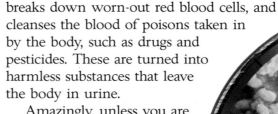

Liver lobules

The liver is made up of six-sided columns called lobules. Branches of the hepatic artery and the hepatic portal vein carry blood to the outer part of each lobule. From here blood passes along spaces called sinusoids, supplying liver cells with oxygen and food to be processed. Treated blood empties into the central branch of the hepatic vein, which carries blood back to the heart.

Branch of hepatic vein

Liver cell

Bile duct

Lobule

Sinusoid

Branch of hepatic artery

Branch of hepatic portal vein

Right lobe of the liver

Left lobe of the liver

Bile duct

Hepatic portal vein (brings blood rich in food from small intestine)

Gall bladder

Hepatic artery (brings oxygen-rich blood from the lungs)

Loads of lobules

Inside the liver, the blood vessels divide into millions of tiny branches that weave in and out of the lobules. Blood brings nutrients from digested food to the lobules, to be processed by the liver cells. The process uses oxygen from the lungs and generates an enormous amount of heat.

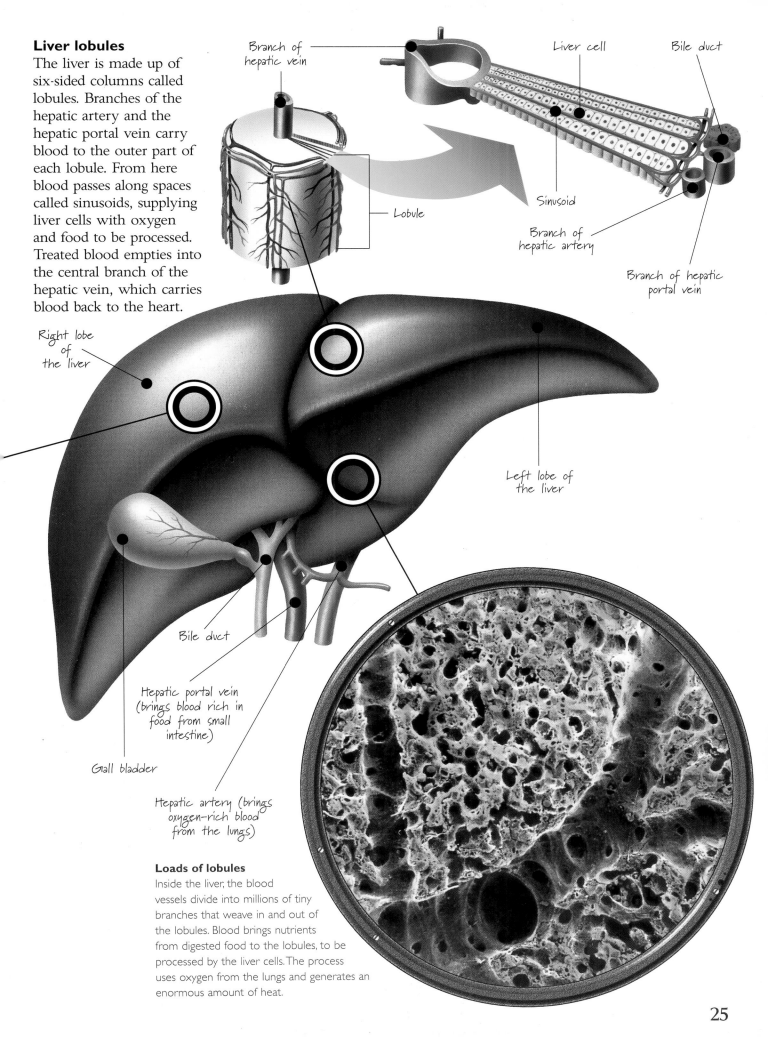

25

The Large Intestine

About 10 hours after you have eaten, a mushy paste of undigested food reaches the large intestine. It may take another 20 hours to pass completely through the body.

The waste material that gathers in the large intestine is called faeces. It consists mostly of dead cells from the gut wall, mucus, the remains of digestive juices, bacteria and some water, as well as hard indigestible bits of food, mainly the fibres from fruit, vegetables and grain. Bacteria in the large intestine produce certain vitamins that are absorbed into the blood; they also produce foul-smelling gases. Water is absorbed into the body through the wall of the large intestine, so that the waste material becomes more solid as it moves slowly towards the rectum. How solid the faeces are depends on how much water is in them. Too much water leads to diarrhoea, but too little leads to constipation.

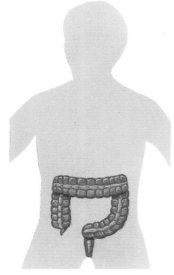

Where is it?
The large intestine is a large tube that coils around the small intestine.

Large intestine

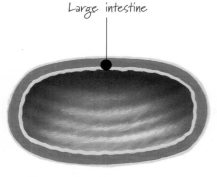

Comparing sizes
The large intestine is just 2 metres (6 feet) long, much shorter than the small intestine. It earns the name 'large' because it is so much wider – 6.5 centimetres (2.5 inches) across. The small intestine measures just 2.5 centimetres (1 inch) across.

Small intestine

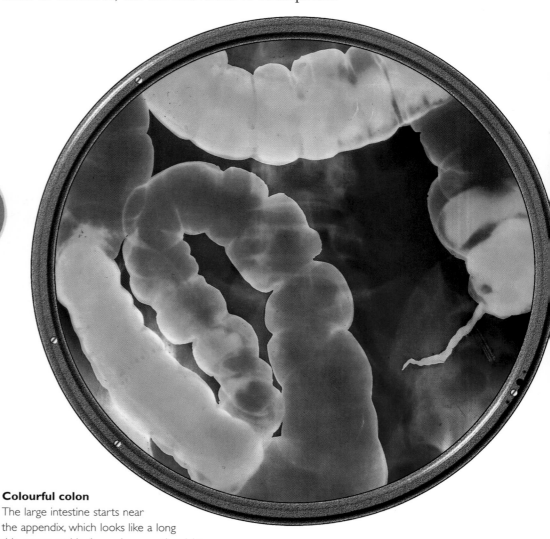

Colourful colon
The large intestine starts near the appendix, which looks like a long thin worm and is shown here on the right, as viewed from behind. The muscular walls of the colon contract behind the undigested food, pushing it slowly towards the rectum.

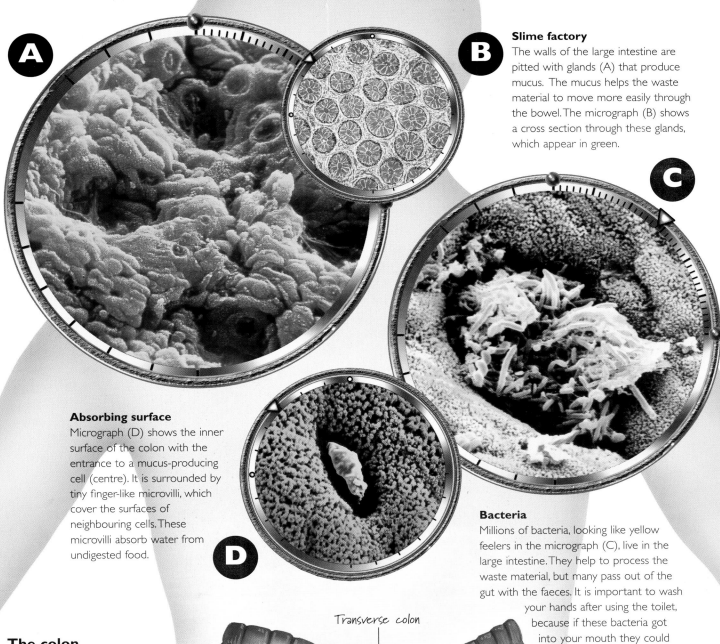

A

B

Slime factory
The walls of the large intestine are pitted with glands (A) that produce mucus. The mucus helps the waste material to move more easily through the bowel. The micrograph (B) shows a cross section through these glands, which appear in green.

C

Absorbing surface
Micrograph (D) shows the inner surface of the colon with the entrance to a mucus-producing cell (centre). It is surrounded by tiny finger-like microvilli, which cover the surfaces of neighbouring cells. These microvilli absorb water from undigested food.

D

Bacteria
Millions of bacteria, looking like yellow feelers in the micrograph (C), live in the large intestine. They help to process the waste material, but many pass out of the gut with the faeces. It is important to wash your hands after using the toilet, because if these bacteria got into your mouth they could make you ill.

The colon
The large intestine is also called the colon. It is divided into three parts — ascending colon, transverse colon and descending colon, so called because they lead up, across and down.

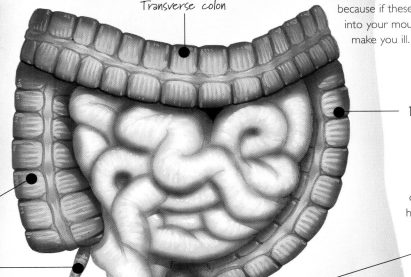

Transverse colon

Descending colon

Rectum
Waste material is stored in the rectal cavity. It moves from here into the rectum just before it leaves the body.

Ascending colon

Appendix
The appendix is the 'tail end' of the large intestine, which humans do not use.

Anus
Two sphincters have to open to allow waste material to leave the body.

USEFUL FOOD

Pre-match meal
Professional footballers often eat pasta a few hours before kick-off. Pasta provides carbohydrate in the form of starch, a vital source of glucose and energy throughout the match.

The body uses three main types of nutrients: carbohydrates, proteins and fats.

Carbohydrates include starch, found in bread, rice and potatoes, and sugars, found in fruit. The main product of carbohydrate digestion is a simple sugar called glucose. This is carried by the blood to all body cells. Inside each cell, glucose combines with oxygen to release energy, which the cell uses to do its work.

Foods such as meat, fish, beans and eggs are rich in proteins. Protein digestion produces building-block molecules called amino acids. Inside cells, these link up to make new proteins for building and repair.

Fats are found in foods such as vegetable oils, meat and dairy products. They are broken down by digestion into fatty acids and glycerol. These are used by cells to provide energy. Fats are also stored under the skin for insulation, and as a protective layer around the internal organs.

Refuelling without stopping
Racing cyclists often drink glucose and water. The glucose is absorbed quickly, giving an instant source of energy.

Body fat

Under your skin is a layer of body fat (left), which is made from eating fat in foods such as oil, eggs, meat and milk. Body fat acts as a protective layer around your internal organs and helps to keep you warm.

Nails and hair

Nails and hair are both made of a protein called keratin. The body builds up proteins such as keratin from proteins in the foods we eat.

ENZYMES

The carbohydrates, fats and proteins we swallow usually enter the digestive system as huge molecules. Outside the body, these molecules can be broken down only at very high temperatures. Cooking often begins the process.

With the help of enzymes, however, food molecules are broken down inside the body at a much lower temperature – about 37 degrees Centigrade (98.6 degrees Fahrenheit). Each enzyme brings about just one kind of chemical reaction, so several different enzymes are needed to digest different kinds of food. Enzymes in the mouth start to digest carbohydrates. But the main work of digestion takes place in the small intestine. Different enzymes from the pancreas and glands in the small intestine work rapidly to break down carbohydrates, proteins and fats. Bile from the liver helps the digestion of fat by breaking it into tiny droplets.

Stomach

Mouth

Stomach

Carbohydrates
The top band shows how enzymes start to work in the mouth, breaking down starch into simple sugars. Carbohydrates are the first foods to be digested and absorbed into the blood.

Proteins
Proteins, shown in the middle band, consist of long chains of amino acids. Enzymes break them down into individual amino acids. Protein digestion begins in the stomach but takes place mainly in the small intestine.

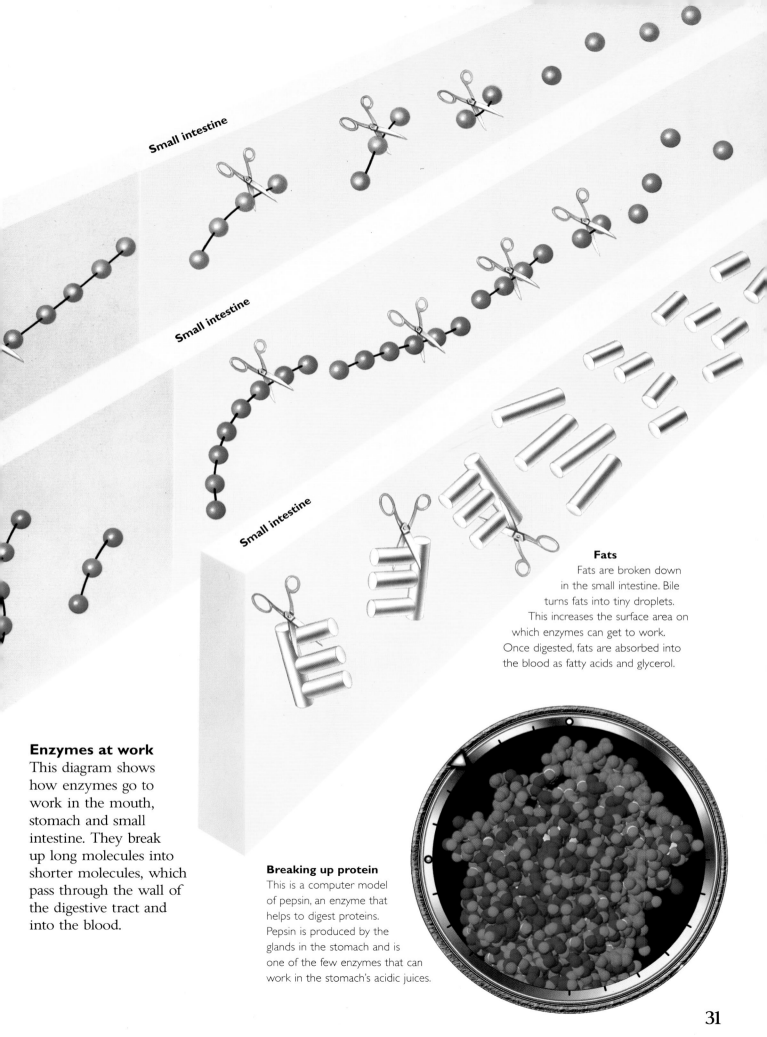

Small intestine

Small intestine

Small intestine

Fats
Fats are broken down in the small intestine. Bile turns fats into tiny droplets. This increases the surface area on which enzymes can get to work. Once digested, fats are absorbed into the blood as fatty acids and glycerol.

Enzymes at work
This diagram shows how enzymes go to work in the mouth, stomach and small intestine. They break up long molecules into shorter molecules, which pass through the wall of the digestive tract and into the blood.

Breaking up protein
This is a computer model of pepsin, an enzyme that helps to digest proteins. Pepsin is produced by the glands in the stomach and is one of the few enzymes that can work in the stomach's acidic juices.

31

VITAMINS, MINERALS & FIBRE

As well as the basic nutrients — proteins, carbohydrates and fats — the body needs small amounts of vitamins and minerals and large amounts of fibre.

Vitamins and minerals are necessary for good health. A balanced diet will provide all the minerals your body needs and more than 12 essential vitamins. Both vitamins and minerals are taken directly into the body and are unchanged by digestion.

Fibre is the indigestible parts of plants — fruit, vegetables and cereals. The digestive system needs large amounts of fibre in order to work properly. Fibre bulks up the waste matter in the large intestine and gives the muscles there something to work against. If your diet doesn't contain enough fibre, the large intestine becomes sluggish and slow, leading to constipation.

Healthy vegetables
Fruit and green vegetables contain many of the essential extras your body needs, such as B vitamins, vitamins C and E, iron and iodine. They are also an excellent source of fibre.

B group vitamins
There are several vitamins in this group. They play many different roles in ensuring that the body's cells work properly. B group vitamins are found in liver, fish, wholegrain cereals and yeast extracts.

Calcium
Milk, cheese and many green vegetables contain calcium. It helps the body form strong bones and teeth. Muscles and nerves also need calcium to work well.

Vital vitamins

Vitamins and minerals keep the body healthy in many different ways. A lack of just one will cause weakness and disease, but luckily everyday foods contain all that the body needs.

Iron

Meat, bread, rice, potatoes and vegetables all contain iron. The body uses iron to make haemoglobin, the substance in red blood cells that carries oxygen around the body.

Vitamin C

Fresh fruit and potatoes are particularly rich in vitamin C, which helps to fight disease and heal wounds.

Potassium

Potassium is absorbed from meat, fish, fruit and vegetables. Like sodium, it is found in the blood and helps to carry nerve impulses.

Sodium

Sodium is obtained from most foods and from table salt (sodium chloride). It forms an important part of body fluids, such as blood, sweat and tears. It also plays a vital role in carrying impulses along nerve fibres.

Vitamin A

Milk, egg yolk and green leafy vegetables contain vitamin A. You need it for healthy skin, eyes, teeth and bones.

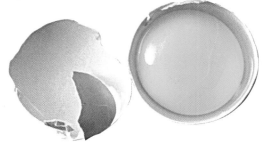

Vitamin D

Vitamin D is contained in oily fish, eggs and margarine. It is also made by the skin using sunlight. Vitamin D helps the bones to use calcium to grow strong.

HEALTHY EATING

A balanced diet is one that gives the body enough energy and all the nutrients it needs to stay fit and healthy. A balanced diet contains many different types of food.

These foods should provide a balance of carbohydrates, proteins and fats, and all the vitamins and minerals needed by the body, as well as fibre and water. Between 55 and 60 per cent of a balanced diet should come from carbohydrates, about 15 per cent from proteins, and about 30 per cent from fats.

The food pyramid opposite shows the proportions in which the main food groups give a balanced diet. Ideally the diet should contain little from group 1, more from group 2 and increasing amounts from groups 3 and 4. If you eat more food than your body can use as energy, the extra is stored as fat. Too many 'junk food' snacks – for example sweets, biscuits and crisps – can provide more sugar and fat than the body needs. Fruit, vegetables and nuts make tasty snacks too.

Tasty prawns
Prawns contain plenty of protein and are rich in a type of fat called cholesterol. Too much cholesterol in the diet may not be good for health.

Fitting the bill
Every meal should provide some energy food, some protein and some fruit or vegetables. Many meals around the world offer a balance of these. This meal includes potato, meat, vegetables, milk and fresh fruit.

Rice dishes
Rice is the most common staple food in the world. Here it will be eaten with stir fry vegetables.

Italian pasta
People in different countries have developed their own style of cooking. Pasta provides the basis for many Italian meals.

Japanese snacks
Japanese snacks (sushi) may include raw fish and vegetables, seaweed and pickles.

Crab's claws
These claws are packed with crab meat that is high in protein and low in fat. Together with this salad, the crab claws provide a nutritious meal.

Exotic fruit
This exotic fruit salad includes kiwi fruit, mango, starfruit, pineapple and banana. Health experts say that we need to eat five portions of fruit and vegetables a day.

1 Foods rich in oils and sugars

2 Protein-rich foods

3 Fresh vegetables and fruit

4 Starchy foods

A pyramid of food
You need to eat more of some kinds of food than others. Bread, potatoes, rice and other staple foods rich in carbohydrates (shown at the bottom) form the basis of any healthy diet. You need only small amounts of sugar and fats (shown at the top).

WATER BALANCE

Dying for a drink
You need to drink at least 1.2 litres (2 pints) of liquid a day. People have survived for two months without food, but cannot live more than a few days without water.

Three-fifths of the body is made up of water. The body's fluids — such as blood, saliva and urine — are mainly water, but all cells including bone, muscle and flesh contain water too.

If you weigh 40 kg (90 lb), your body contains about 24 litres (42 pints) of water. Over a litre of this is lost each day and has to be replaced. Water is lost in several ways. Most is lost as urine, and some in faeces. Water is also lost when you breathe out, through the skin, and by sweating.

All fluids contain water, so much of the lost water is replaced by drinking fluids. Since about half of all food is water, the rest is replaced by eating.

Drenched in sweat
These Sumo wrestlers are working hard to overpower each other. When your muscles work hard, they generate extra heat, which the body needs to lose. Glands in the skin pump out sweat, which you can see on the athlete's arm below. As sweat evaporates, it cools the body down. Even without exercising, you lose about 0.1 litre (0.2 pint) of water every day through your skin.

Water in and water out

You probably lose about 1.2 litres (2 pints) of water each day. Most of this is urine and water lost as sweat through the skin, in faeces and by breathing out. To preserve the amount of water in the body, you must take in at least the same amount as you lose, either by drinking liquids or in your food.

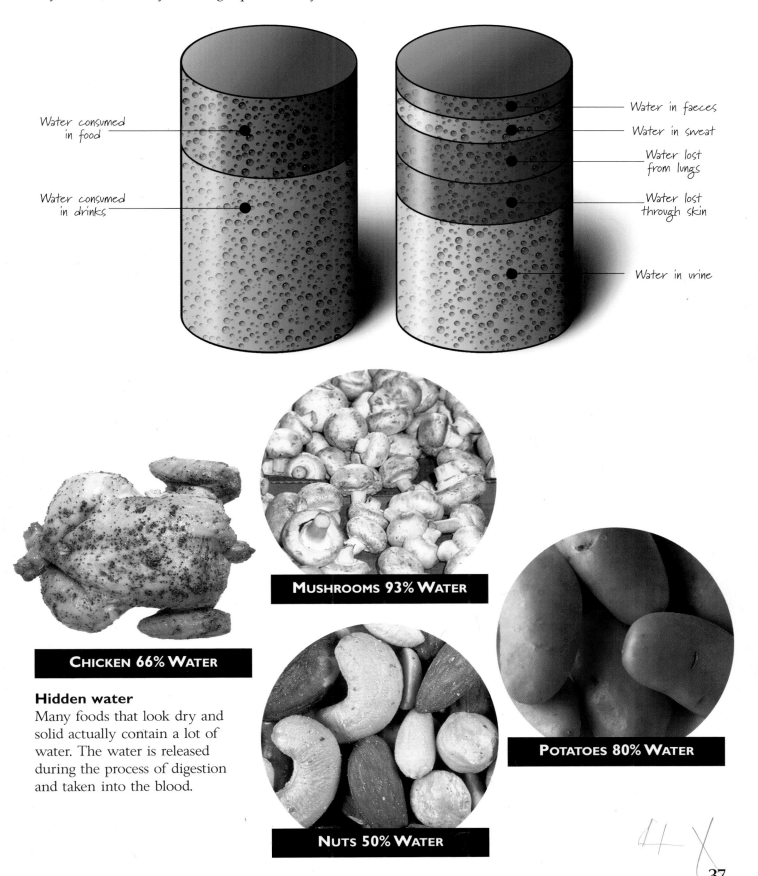

Water consumed in food

Water consumed in drinks

Water in faeces

Water in sweat

Water lost from lungs

Water lost through skin

Water in urine

MUSHROOMS 93% WATER

CHICKEN 66% WATER

POTATOES 80% WATER

Hidden water

Many foods that look dry and solid actually contain a lot of water. The water is released during the process of digestion and taken into the blood.

NUTS 50% WATER

Waterworks

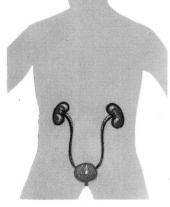

Where are they?
There are two kidneys, one on each side of the body. They lie under the ribs close to the spine. Two tubes lead from the kidneys into the bladder lower down in the abdomen.

Water and salts enter the body in drinks and in food and are absorbed through the walls of the intestine into the blood. It is the kidneys' job to control the amount of water and salts in the blood.

In the kidneys, excess water and salts are extracted from the blood and sent to the bladder. If you eat very salty foods, the kidneys need extra water to get rid of the excess salt. When there is too much salt or too little water in the blood, the inside of the mouth becomes drier and you feel thirsty. This prompts you to drink more fluids to restore the balance of water and salts in the body.

The kidneys have another role. They are a complex filtering system that cleans the blood. As blood passes through them, wastes such as urea are dissolved in water to make urine, which is sent to the bladder.

Urine drain
Urine drains from the kidneys, shown in the X-ray on the right in green, and trickles along tubes that funnel into the ureters, shown in red. Visible between the ureters is the spine.

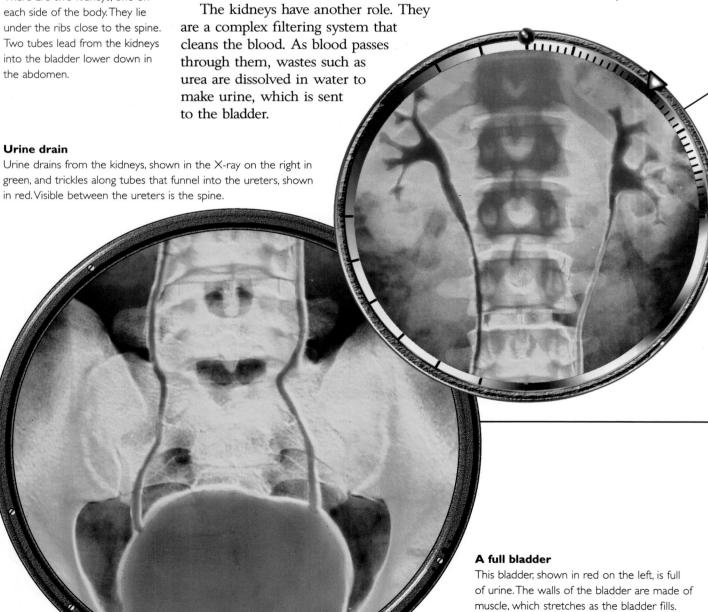

A full bladder
This bladder, shown in red on the left, is full of urine. The walls of the bladder are made of muscle, which stretches as the bladder fills. The muscles relax again when you urinate and empty the bladder.

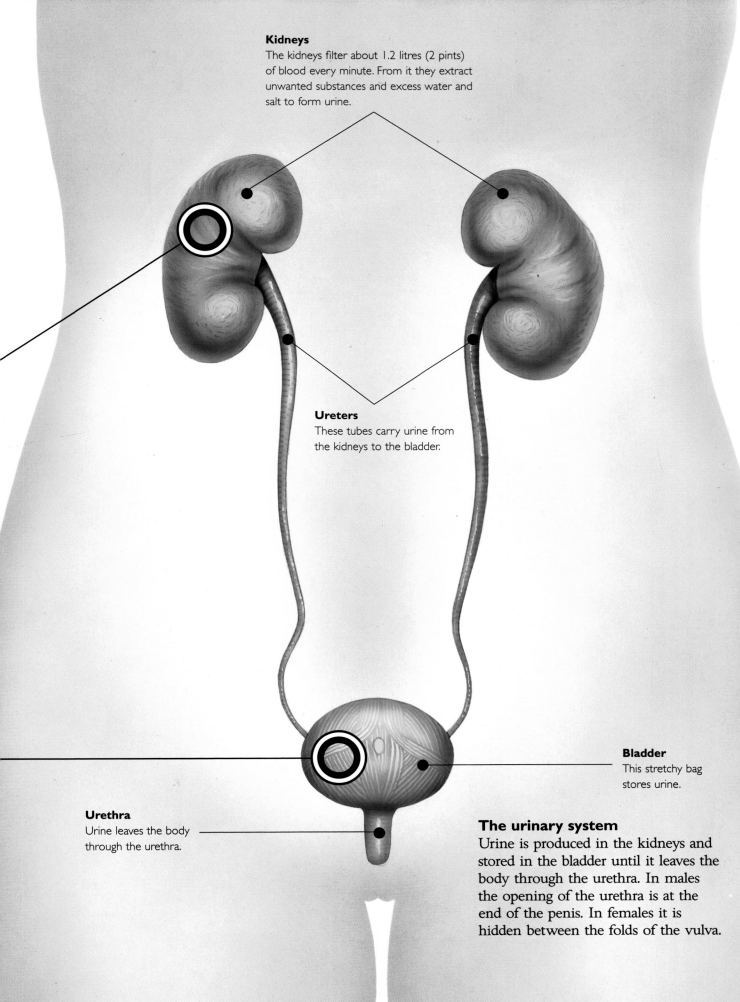

Kidneys
The kidneys filter about 1.2 litres (2 pints) of blood every minute. From it they extract unwanted substances and excess water and salt to form urine.

Ureters
These tubes carry urine from the kidneys to the bladder.

Bladder
This stretchy bag stores urine.

Urethra
Urine leaves the body through the urethra.

The urinary system

Urine is produced in the kidneys and stored in the bladder until it leaves the body through the urethra. In males the opening of the urethra is at the end of the penis. In females it is hidden between the folds of the vulva.

THE KIDNEYS

The kidneys clean the blood by passing it through tiny filters called nephrons. Each kidney has over a million nephrons, so between them, the kidneys can filter about a quarter of your blood every minute.

Blood arrives in the kidneys under great pressure, because it is pumped there straight from the heart. As blood enters a nephron, water and everything dissolved in it — including food, salts and waste products such as urea — is forced out of the blood into tiny tubules. As these substances pass along the tubule, most of the water and all the things the body wants to keep are filtered back through the walls of the tubule into the blood. The waste products and some of the water continue to flow along the tubule to the ureter, and so into the bladder. The cleansed blood leaves the kidney and continues its journey round the body.

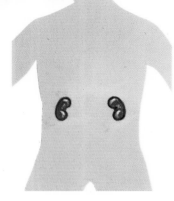

Where are they?
To find exactly where the kidneys are, stand with your hands by your sides. Your kidneys are in the middle of your back at the same level as your elbows.

Inside the kidney
The knots of tiny coiling tubes shown in red are glomeruli. Each one is linked to a nephron. Liquid leaves the blood, passes through the glomeruli and into the nephrons. There it is filtered and turned into urine.

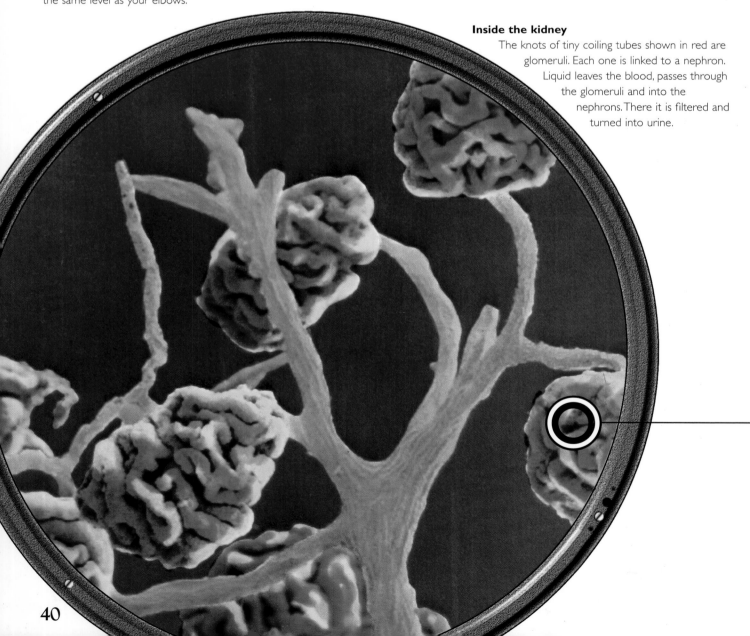

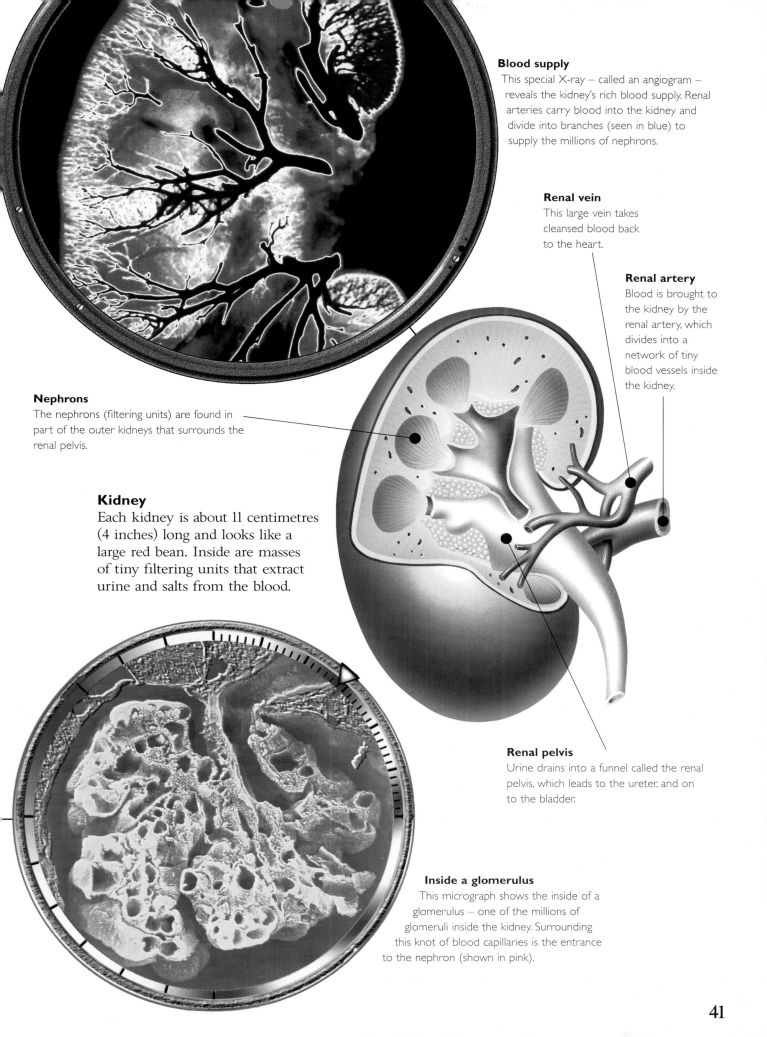

Blood supply
This special X-ray – called an angiogram – reveals the kidney's rich blood supply. Renal arteries carry blood into the kidney and divide into branches (seen in blue) to supply the millions of nephrons.

Renal vein
This large vein takes cleansed blood back to the heart.

Renal artery
Blood is brought to the kidney by the renal artery, which divides into a network of tiny blood vessels inside the kidney.

Nephrons
The nephrons (filtering units) are found in part of the outer kidneys that surrounds the renal pelvis.

Kidney
Each kidney is about 11 centimetres (4 inches) long and looks like a large red bean. Inside are masses of tiny filtering units that extract urine and salts from the blood.

Renal pelvis
Urine drains into a funnel called the renal pelvis, which leads to the ureter, and on to the bladder.

Inside a glomerulus
This micrograph shows the inside of a glomerulus – one of the millions of glomeruli inside the kidney. Surrounding this knot of blood capillaries is the entrance to the nephron (shown in pink).

THE BLADDER

Most of the water that passes through the kidneys is returned to the blood. But every day about 1 to 1.5 litres (1.7 to 2.5 pints) trickles down to the bladder as urine.

The bladder can hold only between 150 and 600 ml (0.25 to 1 pint) of urine. This is why you have to empty it several times a day. The amount of urine your body produces in a day depends on a number of things, such as how hot the weather is and how much liquid you drink. If more water leaves the body as sweat, less urine is produced. This urine is more concentrated. It contains the same amount of urea, but less water. If you drink a lot of liquid, your body will produce more urine, but it will be less concentrated.

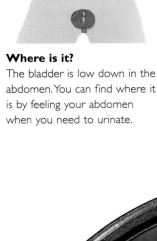

Where is it?
The bladder is low down in the abdomen. You can find where it is by feeling your abdomen when you need to urinate.

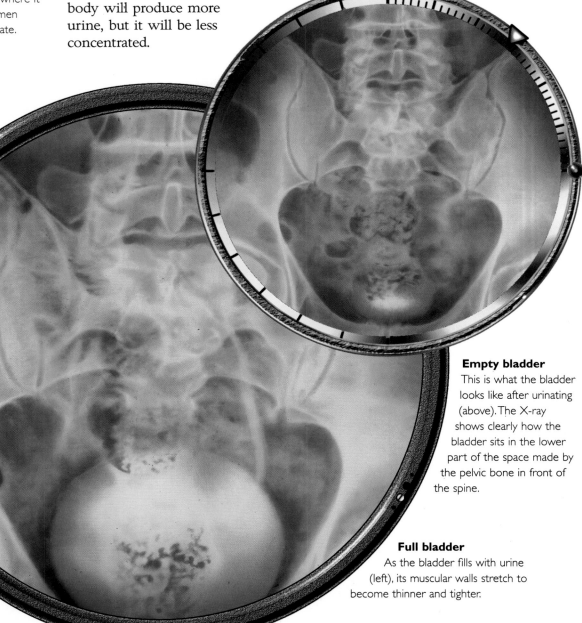

Empty bladder
This is what the bladder looks like after urinating (above). The X-ray shows clearly how the bladder sits in the lower part of the space made by the pelvic bone in front of the spine.

Full bladder
As the bladder fills with urine (left), its muscular walls stretch to become thinner and tighter.

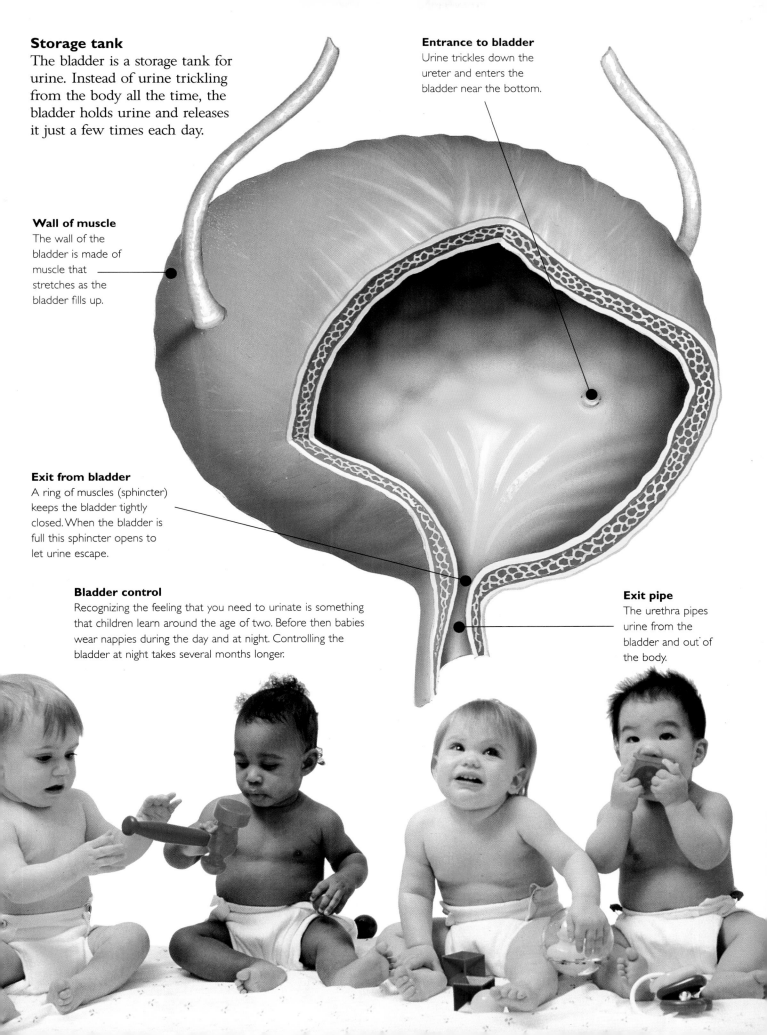

Storage tank
The bladder is a storage tank for urine. Instead of urine trickling from the body all the time, the bladder holds urine and releases it just a few times each day.

Entrance to bladder
Urine trickles down the ureter and enters the bladder near the bottom.

Wall of muscle
The wall of the bladder is made of muscle that stretches as the bladder fills up.

Exit from bladder
A ring of muscles (sphincter) keeps the bladder tightly closed. When the bladder is full this sphincter opens to let urine escape.

Bladder control
Recognizing the feeling that you need to urinate is something that children learn around the age of two. Before then babies wear nappies during the day and at night. Controlling the bladder at night takes several months longer.

Exit pipe
The urethra pipes urine from the bladder and out of the body.

WHEN THINGS GO WRONG

When the digestive tract works smoothly, you hardly notice it, but sometimes things go wrong.

Most stomach aches are simply caused by too much air or gas in the stomach. But vomiting or diarrhoea may be triggered by germs that get into the body with your food. The food itself may be contaminated, or the things you are eating with may be dirty.

The best way to avoid food poisoning is to keep food clean and wash your hands before touching food.

Some people suffer from food allergies. Certain kinds of food can make them sick or cause a rash. Many processed foods have chemicals added to them to make them look better or last longer. These chemicals are often blamed for allergies, and some additives may even cause long-term health problems. However, normally healthy foods such as cheese, eggs, peanuts and seafood can cause allergies too.

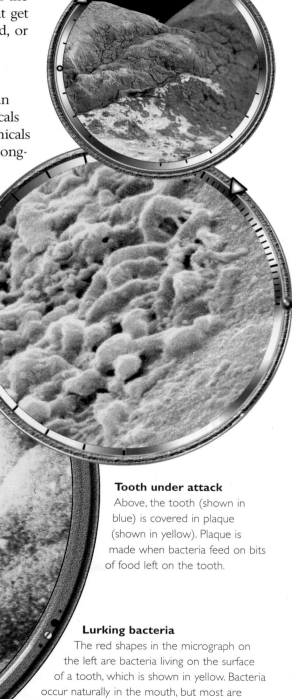

Tooth decay
In the micrograph below, the bacteria in the plaque (shown in brown) have produced acid that is making a hole in the enamel covering the tooth.

Tooth under attack
Above, the tooth (shown in blue) is covered in plaque (shown in yellow). Plaque is made when bacteria feed on bits of food left on the tooth.

Lurking bacteria
The red shapes in the micrograph on the left are bacteria living on the surface of a tooth, which is shown in yellow. Bacteria occur naturally in the mouth, but most are brushed away when you clean your teeth.

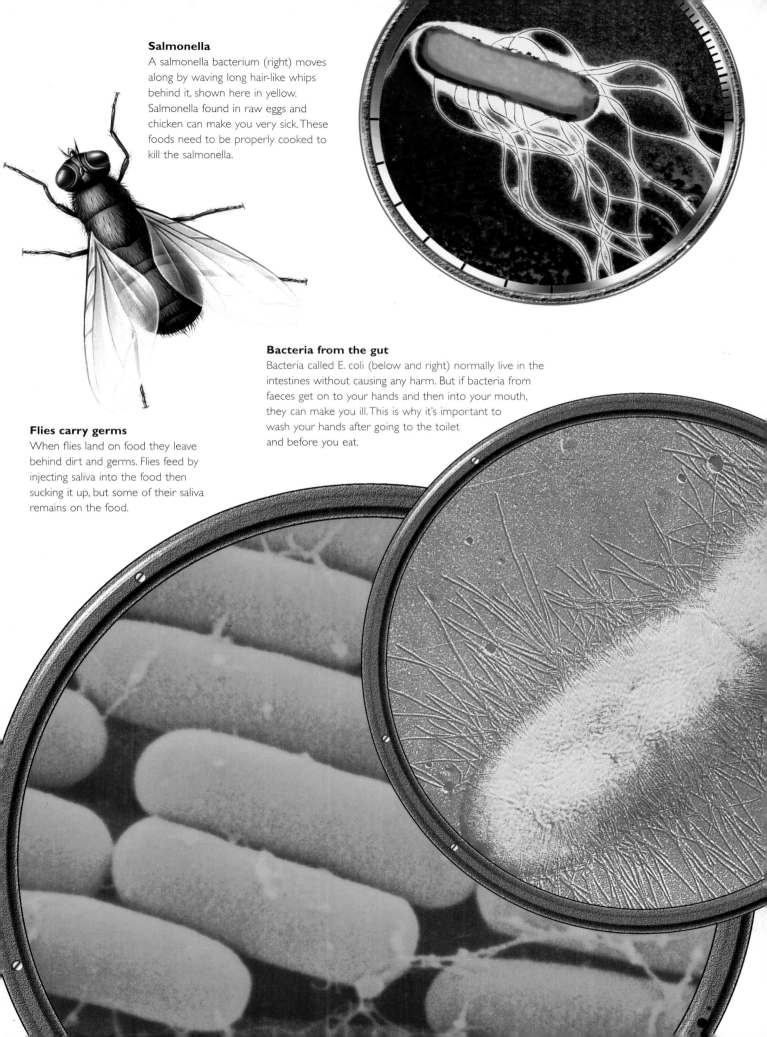

Salmonella
A salmonella bacterium (right) moves along by waving long hair-like whips behind it, shown here in yellow. Salmonella found in raw eggs and chicken can make you very sick. These foods need to be properly cooked to kill the salmonella.

Flies carry germs
When flies land on food they leave behind dirt and germs. Flies feed by injecting saliva into the food then sucking it up, but some of their saliva remains on the food.

Bacteria from the gut
Bacteria called E. coli (below and right) normally live in the intestines without causing any harm. But if bacteria from faeces get on to your hands and then into your mouth, they can make you ill. This is why it's important to wash your hands after going to the toilet and before you eat.

GLOSSARY

ALLERGY
Exaggerated response of the body's immune system to a substance or material that does not normally affect people.

AMINO ACID
A building block of protein. Protein in food is broken down into amino acids during digestion and then reassembled into new proteins in the body.

ANTISEPTIC
A substance that kills bacteria.

ANUS
The opening at the end of the digestive tract through which faeces leave the body.

BACTERIA
Microscopic living things, some kinds of which can cause disease. Some bacteria cause food poisoning.

BLADDER
A stretchy bag with a muscular wall that collects and stores urine.

BILE
A yellow-green liquid that helps break down fats in the small intestine. Bile is made in the liver and stored in the gall bladder.

CARBOHYDRATE
Substance that is an important source of energy. Simple carbohydrates, or sugars, include glucose. Complex carbohydrates, such as starch, are found in bread, pasta, rice and potatoes. Starch is broken down into glucose during digestion.

CELL
The body's building block. Each part of the body, such as the liver, heart, skin and bones, is made up of millions of cells.

DUODENUM
The first part of the small intestine.

ENZYME
A chemical that takes part in chemical changes in the body without being changed itself. Different enzymes help to break down and digest different kinds of food.

FAECES
Undigested waste that passes through the large intestine and leaves the body through the anus.

FAT
Substance that is source of energy and is also used by the body to insulate it and keep it warm. Dairy products, red meat and vegetable oils are all rich in fats.

FATTY ACIDS
Substances that combine with glycerol to make fat.

FIBRE
Plant material that passes undigested through the gut. Vegetables, fruit, wholemeal bread and brown rice are rich in fibre.

GALL BLADDER
Small bag or sac in which bile is stored.

GASTRIC JUICE
Digestive juice produced by the glands in the lining of the stomach.

GLAND
An organ or part of the body that produces something useful, such as digestive juice, sweat or a hormone.

GLUCOSE
A type of sugar produced when carbohydrates are digested. Within each body cell, glucose combines with oxygen to produce energy.

GLYCEROL
One of the substances that make up fat.

GLYCOGEN
The form in which glucose is stored in the liver and muscles. Glycogen is changed back into glucose when the level of glucose in the blood drops.

INTESTINES
This tube joins the stomach to the anus.

KIDNEYS
Two organs that cleanse the blood, filtering out waste and excess water and salt.

NEPHRON
A filtering unit in the kidney.

OESOPHAGUS
The pipe that takes food from the mouth and throat to the stomach.

PALATE
The roof of the mouth. It is hard at the front and soft at the back of the mouth.

PANCREAS
A large gland which produces digestive juices containing several enzymes.

PERISTALSIS
Contractions of the muscles in the oesophagus and intestines that squeeze food through the digestive tract.

PROTEIN
Substance that the body needs to grow and to repair and maintain cells. Fish, eggs, cheese, meat and beans are all rich in proteins.

SPHINCTER
A ring of muscles that opens and closes an opening in the body.

STARCH
A carbohydrate made in plants and broken down during digestion to become glucose.

TUBULE
A long tube that forms part of a nephron, the kidneys' filtering unit.

UREA
Waste substance made in the liver and filtered out of the blood in the kidneys.

URINE
A liquid made of urea and other waste substances dissolved in water. Urine is produced in the kidneys and stored in the bladder.

VALVE
A device that allows liquid or gas to flow in one direction only.

VILLUS/VILLI
Tiny projections in the intestines through which digested food is absorbed into the blood.

INDEX

Acknowledgements

The publishers wish to thank the following for supplying photographs for this book: Biophoto Associates/Science Photo Library (SPL) back cover (BR), 41(TL); Dr Tony . Brain/SPL 44 (CR), 45 (B); BSIP VEM/SPL 14 (B), 15 (TR); Scott Camazine/SPL 6 (B); Prof. S Cinti, Universite d'Ancone, CNRI/SPL 4 (C), 13 (BL), 23 (BL), 29 (TL), 40 (BL); Clinical Radiology Dept, Salisbury District Hospital/SPL 2 (BR), 21 (BL), 23 (TR), 42 (C, BL); CNRI/SPL front cover (TL, CR), 19 (C, TL), 26 (C), 27 (TL), 38 (CR, BL), 45 (CR); A B Dowsett/SPL front cover (CL), 19 (BL); Eye of Science/SPL 44 (TR); Cecil H Fox/SPL 27 (TC); Gca–CNRI/SPL 6 (TL); John Heseltine 34 (TR); Mehau Kulyk/SPL 16 (TR), 17 (BR); Dick Luria/SPL 36 (BR); Astrid and Hanns-Frieder Michler/SPL 23 (TL); Miles Kelly Archives 4 (TR), 9 (CR), 28 (TL, CL,), 28-9 (B), 32 (CL, CR, BL), 33 (TR, C, B), 34 (TL, CR) 35 (TL, CL,), 37 (BL, BC, BR); Prof. P Motta/Dept of Anatomy/University 'La Sapienza', Rome/SPL, front cover (CL), 6 (CL), 19 (BL), 3 (CR, B), 20 (CR), 11 (TR), 12 (BL, BC,), 13 (C), 24 (B), 25 (B), 27 (TR); Profs P Motta and T Naguro/SPL 22 (C); Profs P M Motta, T Fujita and M Muto/SPL 24 (C); Profs P Motta, K R Porter and P M Andrews/SPL 7; NASA/SPL 17 (T); Alfred Pasieka/SPL 16 (TR); Quest/SPL 27 (C); Rex Features London 36 (CR); Dr R F R Schiller/SPL 18 (C); SPL 21 (B), 44 (BL), 31 (BR); Secchi, Lecaque, Roussel, UCLAF–CNRI/SPL 41 (BL); Pat Spillane 8 (TL, model Alex Bermingham; C, model Puspita McKenzie; BL, model Wesley Stevenson; BR, model Eriko Sato), 9 (B, model Puspita Mckenzie), 12 (TL, model Alex Bermingham), 14 (L, model Shoji Tanaka), 29 (TR, model Eriko Sato; CR), 34 (BL, model Chloe Boulton), 36 (L, model Laura Saunter); The Stock Market, 34 (BR), 35 (TR), 43 (B); Usda/SPL 45 (TR).